The Essential Douglas LePan

The Essential Douglas LePan

selected by John Barton

The Porcupine's Quill

Library and Archives Canada Cataloguing in Publication

Title: The essential Douglas LePan / selected by John Barton.
Other titles: Poems. Selections
Names: LePan, Douglas, 1914–1998, author. | Barton, John, 1957– editor.
Series: Essential poets (Erin, Ont.) ; 19.
Description: Series statement: Essential poets series ; 19 | Includes index.
Identifiers: Canadiana 20189067535 | ISBN 9780889844230 (softcover)
Classification: LCC PS8523.E67 A6 2019 | DDC C811/.54—dc23

1 2 3 • 21 20 19

Published by The Porcupine's Quill, 68 Main Street, PO Box 160,
Erin, Ontario N0B 1T0. http://porcupinesquill.ca

Copyedited by Chandra Wohleber.
Represented in Canada by Canadian Manda.
Trade orders are available from University of Toronto Press.

We acknowledge the support of the Ontario Arts Council and the Canada Council for the Arts for our publishing program. The financial support of the Government of Canada through the Canada Book Fund is also gratefully acknowledged.

Canada Council for the Arts | Conseil des arts du Canada
ONTARIO ARTS COUNCIL
CONSEIL DES ARTS DE L'ONTARIO
an Ontario government agency
un organisme du gouvernement de l'Ontario
Canada
Ontario
Ontario Media Development Corporation

Table of Contents

Foreword

In January 2004, during my first week as editor, *The Malahat Review* received a submission of poems by Douglas LePan. I was astonished. It's not often the editor of a literary journal is offered the opportunity, as I was by Don LePan, the poet's son, to consider posthumous work by an important, if neglected poet. A measure of this neglect is the degree to which I had to convince the magazine's poetry board of the merits of publishing late work by a poet whom readers might know only through several chronically anthologized poems. We ultimately accepted three of the poems that LePan's son had submitted. At the board's request, I added a note explaining why work so clearly 'anachronistic' deserved a contemporary audience.

Born in 1914, LePan truly was a well-rounded intellectual, having been educated at the University of Toronto and Oxford. At the beginning of the Second World War, he worked in England as a civilian for the Canadian Army and at the Canadian High Commission. As soon as he could, he made 'an honest man'[1] of himself by enlisting and serving in Italy: 'I will remember till my dying day all those artillery positions for the attack on Cassio,' he acknowledges in the introduction to his memoir, *Bright Glass of Memory*, 'and the crossing of the Rapido, and the breaking of the Hitler Line, and during the pursuit to Rome, when the regiment took up a new position almost every day and when the air was jewelled with the Italian light and the constant danger of death.'[2]

The tension between the calm, but war-devastated Italian countryside and the dangers that the Canadian troops face gives *The Net and the Sword* (1953), LePan's second book of poetry, its disturbing poignancy. In 'Tuscan Villa', he describes the abandoned country house where his unit had dug in as an 'Unblinking sphinx with the sunlight goring its flanks / The villa stares over the undulant plain / Past the new-made graves and the tanks upturned like

1. Douglas LePan, *Bright Glass of Memory: A Set of Four Memoirs*. Toronto: McGraw-Hill Ryerson, 1979, 3.
2. Ibid, 4.

beetles / Past the poplars dozing in the river-valley / And the flickering, fiery tongues of the olive trees.'

Landscape caught LePan's eye from the beginning of his writing career. In *The Wounded Prince and Other Poems* (1948), the Canadian wilderness figures prominently, not only in two of his best-known poems, '*Coureurs de bois*' and 'A Country Without a Mythology', but also in 'Canoe-Trip'. The latter recounts an afternoon of paddling through scenery worthy of the Group of Seven: 'What of this fabulous country / Now that we have it reduced to a few hot hours / And sun-burn on our backs? / On this south side the countless archipelagoes, / The slipway where titans sent splashing the last great glaciers … / Into this reservoir we dipped and pulled out lakes and rivers, / We strung them together and made our circuit.' Tuscany and Ontario lake country may be described with the same feeling for beauty, but the experiences figured against them couldn't be more different. In 'The Green Man', from *Something Still to Find* (1982), landscape and figure seem almost to merge: 'Leaves twist out of his mouth, of his eyes, of his ears, / twine down over his thighs, spring out of his heels, / as he runs through the woods as a deer or an outlaw, or curled / up in moss and bracken, light speckling him feckless, / he watches the other animals, himself hidden / like an animal, although so strangely human.' The 'strangeness' of being human, with the human capacity for violence as well as for unstinting civility, is the figure metaphorically running through LePan's cosmos in many guises.

One guise of course is LePan himself and how, as a poet, he has chosen to be seen and to see himself. As M. Travis Lane points out in a review of *Weathering It: Complete Poems 1948–1987* that appeared in *The Fiddlehead* in 1989, LePan can be a groomed autobiographical poet: 'the self-image is all-important, not just as subject … but as style itself.'[3] The title suite of the fifty sonnets, which prefaces the complete contents of his first three books, showcases his subtle mastery of prosody. Having turned seventy-three the year the book was published, he deploys multiple technical effects to give this overview of his life from childhood to old age a beguiling patina. For

3. M. Travis Lane, 'Imagining a Hero', *The Fiddlehead* 159 (Spring 1989): 107.

LePan, polish, like good morals and honesty, is key to personality. An example of the verse memoir, 'Weathering It' is rivalled by few written since.

In *Far Voyages* (1990), LePan took the impulse for self-revelation a step further by coming out in his poetry as a gay man at age seventy-six. A suite of love poems, the collection is dedicated to the memory of a much younger lover, who died in 1985. The frankness of these poems encourages the reader to wade into homoerotic currents previously unremarked-upon in earlier work, which I imagine he must have composed with painstaking circumspection. LePan proposes in his memoir, *Bright Glass of Memory* (1979), that the poetry of T.S. Eliot, whom he knew during and immediately after the Second World War, cannot be fully understood divorced from the details of his life, despite Eliot's assertions that such readings must be proscribed. As LePan developed his argument, he cannot have failed to have had the people and the circumstances that had inspired his own dissembling poems of the forties and fifties front of mind. In 1979, could he have guessed that he would publish a book as candid as *Far Voyages* eleven years later, knowing also how it would alter the appreciation of his past and future work? 'Deny, or seem to deny, the connection between the poem and the loam of the poet's life and experience,' LePan offers, 'and you may rob it of much of its savour and of much of its power to nourish, leaving it dry and synthetic.'[4] The poems in the Spring 2004 issue of *The Malahat Review* more openly sketch same-sex desire's once-hidden contours. When I first read 'On a Path Behind the Hotel', I recognized its setting immediately as Majors' Hill Park, which, from behind the Chateau Laurier, looks across the Rideau Canal to Parliament Hill. Men have cruised for sex there since before Confederation. A younger LePan may have 'lived' this poem; he doubtless knew men who did.

If a single theme unifies LePan's work, it is the ubiquity of the hero. In the *coureurs de bois* of *The Wounded Prince*, the soldiers of *The Net and the Sword*, and the green man running through the woods of *Something Still to Find*, he sees qualities that make them

4. Lane, 'Imagining a Hero', 136.

worthy of fealty. In *Macalister, or Dying in the Dark* (1995), a verse drama with five principal voices, LePan articulates his final, most fleshed-out portrait of a hero. An acquaintance from the poet's undergraduate years at the University of Toronto, John Kenneth Macalister, was captured as a spy in occupied France, imprisoned and savagely executed. As characterized by LePan, Macalister grieves his own foreshortened life with stoicism. Heroism, for LePan, plays out in moments of intimacy as well. The beloved is esteemed as much for his audacity and moral strength as for tenderness and fineness of form. 'So the parts are evenly divided between us, dear comrade-in-arms[,]' he offers in 'According to La Rochefoucauld', 'But my part is far easier than yours. I'm constantly finding / in you new things to love, new drolleries, new endurances. / While you? / Free as you are, and as I want you to be, / I'm afraid there must be many times when constancy for you / comes down to a point of honour.'

LePan's finest traits as a poet are discretion and candour. They afford him poise in the face of any ordeal that life presents — from war and nation-building to issues of love — and allow him to demonstrate his own courage. Like the men he admires, he endeavours to rise to each adversity, not because he's convinced success is inevitable (the narrator of 'Weathering It' itemizes his failings), but because, as circumstances permit, honesty is required. For decades, homophobia had caused him to hide who he was behind the polish of his poems. *Far Voyages*, written in the closing chapters of a career that needed no further embellishment, stands as a landmark. He may have entered into the conversation about queer agency late, but he ennobled it nevertheless, by speaking publicly for the very first time. The poet of *Far Voyages* also causes us to rethink his past work. We have come to realize he had been speaking truthfully, albeit carefully, in concert with his other themes, for a very long time.

—John Barton

The Wounded Prince

In the eye is the wound.

Lancings of pity, blades of sensual disappointment
Have pierced the delicate pupil.
Transfixed, the bird of heavenly airs
Is struck at sundown,
Entering the leafy wood, under the heavy lintel.

Gathered in that point all sharp humiliations;
The strokes converge.
The feathered dreams fly home from fruitless voyages.
Light needles.
Still to and fro they hawk their costliest plumage.

In your dear eye....

The dark scar sings from the wanton thicket
Its princely grief;
Sets up in perilous leaves the crest of bravery;
Impaled, sings on;
Will not disown its fettering crest and crown;

So that what never could be dreamt of has been made.
From target's puny eye
Such liquid compass of this wide, aerial gaze;
From wounds, from wounds
By love inflicted, this strict and healing blade.

Coureurs de bois

Thinking of you, I think of the *coureurs de bois,*
Swarthy men grown almost to savage size
Who put their brown wrists through the arras of the woods
And were lost — sometimes for months. Word would come back:
One had been seen in Crêve-coeur, deserted and starving,
One at Sault Sainte Marie shouldering the rapids.
Giant-like, their labours stalked the streets of Quebec
Though they themselves had dwindled in distance: names only;
Rumours; quicksilvery spies into nature's secrets;
Rivers that seldom ran in the sun. Their resource
Would sparkle and then flow back under clouds of hemlock.

So you should have travelled with them. Or with La Salle.
He could feed his heart with the heart of a continent,
Insatiate, how noble a wounded animal,
Who sought for his wounds the balsam of adventure,
The sap from some deep, secret tree. But now
That the forests are cut down, the rivers charted,
Where can you turn, where can you travel? Unless
Through the desperate wilderness behind your eyes,
So full of falls and glooms and desolations,
Disasters I have glimpsed but few would dream of,
You seek new Easts. The coats of difficult honour,
Bright with brocaded birds and curious flowers,
Stowed so long with vile packs of pemmican,
Futile, weighing you down on slippery portages,
Would flutter at last in the courts of a clement country,
Where the air is silken, the manners easy,
Under a guiltless and reconciling sun.

You hesitate. The trees are entangled with menace.
The voyage is perilous into the dark interior.
But then your hands go to the thwarts. You smile. And so
I watch you vanish in a wood of heroes,
Wild Hamlet with the features of Horatio.

A Country Without a Mythology

No monuments or landmarks guide the stranger
Going among this savage people, masks
Taciturn or babbling out an alien jargon
And moody as barbaric skies are moody.

Berries must be his food. Hurriedly
He shakes the bushes, plucks pickerel from the river,
Forgetting every grace and ceremony,
Feeds like an Indian, and is on his way.

And yet, for all his haste, time is worth nothing.
The abbey clock, the dial in the garden,
Fade like saint's days and festivals.
Months, years, are here unbroken virgin forests.

There is no law — even no atmosphere
To smooth the anger of the flagrant sun.
November skies sting, sting like icicles.
The land is open to all violent weathers.

Passion is not more quick. Lightnings in August
Stagger, rocks split, tongues in the forest hiss,
As fire drinks up the lovely sea-dream coolness.
This is the land the passionate man must travel.

Sometimes — perhaps at the tentative fall of twilight —
A belief will settle that waiting around the bend
Are sanctities of childhood, that melting birds
Will sing him into a limpid gracious Presence.

The hills will fall in folds, the wilderness
Will be a garment innocent and lustrous
To wear upon a birthday, under a light
That curls and smiles, a golden-haired Archangel.

And now the channel opens. But nothing alters.
Mile after mile of tangled struggling roots,
Wild-rice, stumps, weeds, that clutch at the canoe,
Wild birds hysterical in tangled trees.

And not a sign, no emblem in the sky
Or boughs to friend him as he goes; for who
Will stop where, clumsily constructed, daubed
With war-paint, teeters some lust-red Manitou?

Canoe-Trip

What of this fabulous country
Now that we have it reduced to a few hot hours
And sun-burn on our backs?
On this south side the countless archipelagoes,
The slipway where titans sent splashing the last great glaciers;
And then up to the foot of the blue pole star
A wilderness,
The pinelands whose limits seem distant as Thule,
The millions of lakes once cached and forgotten,
The clearings enamelled with blue blueberries, rank silence about them;
And skies that roll all day with cloud-chimeras
To baffle the eye with portents and unwritten myths,
The flames of sunset, the lions of gold and gules.
Into this reservoir we dipped and pulled out lakes and rivers,
We strung them together and made our circuit.
Now what shall be our word as we return,
What word of this curious country?

It is good,
It is a good stock to own though it seldom pays dividends.
There are holes here and there for a gold-mine or a hydro-plant.

But the tartan of river and rock spreads undisturbed,
The plaid of a land with little desire to buy or sell.
The dawning light skirls out its independence;
At noon the brazen trumpets slash the air;
Night falls, the gulls scream sharp defiance;
Let whoever comes to tame this land, beware!
Can you put a bit to the lunging wind?
Can you hold wild horses by the hair?
Then have no hope to harness the energy here,
It gallops along the wind away.
But here are crooked nerves made straight,

The fracture cured no doctor could correct.
The hand and mind, reknit, stand whole for work;
The fable proves no cul-de-sac.
Now from the maze we circle back;
The map suggested a wealth of cloudy escapes;
That was a dream, we have converted the dream to act.
And what we now expect is not simplicity,
No steady breeze, or any surprise,
Orchids along the portage, white water, crimson leaves.
Content, we face again the complex task.

And yet the marvels we have seen remain.
We think of the eagles, of the fawns at the river bend,
The storms, the sudden sun, the clouds sheered downwards.
O so to move! With such immaculate decision!
O proudly as waterfalls curling like cumulus!

Tuscan Villa

As the winds veer
The weathervane smiles
But the bell in the lofty belfry
No longer tells the hour
In the sunlight perfect as a tear.
And, if it did,
Would the soldiers crunching the tiles,
Would the soldiers listen
Or the doves that under the broad eaves harbour?

Unblinking sphinx with the sunlight goring its flanks
The villa stares over the undulant plain
Past the new-made graves and the tanks upturned like beetles
Past the poplars dozing in the river-valley
And the flickering, fiery tongues of the olive trees
Hazily, to where a cypressed campanile
Or rosy duomo has become irrelevant fuzz
In a pair of binoculars, too dim to provide the guns
With a reference-object or add to a new triangulation.
But there at the periphery persists some old
Enigma, exhaled long ago like a smile or a gesture,
That the villa dallies with, dallies and drops,
In dotage forgetting the key to its own conundrum.
Embrowned with the years, embrasured, bastioned,
It has lost the key down a well or left it in
A bricked-up casemate, and is now too old, too torpid
To care. Explosions seep through the thick walls as rumours.
What little is left of the villa's heart beats slow,
Integuments hardening inwards, all orifices
Closing. Daydreaming towards its end,
How should it hear that the plain is swelling and heaving,
That not far off shells are spouting like whales,
That the landscape is shifting; how should it know
That its own walls have become only
Scaffolding for artillery observations,
Its tower the platform for a survey of destruction?

The straw-thin winds
That float over the tower
Are grist to the grating weathervane
As it cockily struts and grins.
Why is it strange, it creaks, for one species of power
To follow another?
The end of an age,
And the end of an afternoon
Are one and the same to grinding fortune.

Unfortunate order; the architecture of a flower
That drew from the rooted peasants oil and wine
To be involved in the whorled extravagance
Of gallery, chapel, chamber, tower and orchard,
Folding their deep splendours privily
To hide a few in vivid leaves of light.
Music was here; and at a time of festival
Four seasons seemed to circle round a maypole
Streamered with joys that the dancers twirled and untwirled
In the candid light exulting. But not for joys
And feast-days only accompaniment stood by.
Before the music stopped, the flower grew blowsy,
Resided in these spaces resonance
Waiting to catch and liquefy each heart-beat;
The chapel soothed and purified remorse;
Under the entrance-arch regret like a cry
Could curl, as the coachman (huzza!) drove off with a flourish;
Emblems of victorious pride and death
Went echoing through the garden — green laurel leaves
And peacocks — as aids to meditation; a belvedere
Announced the prospect of a lucid future
Where rows of cypresses as confidants
Sponged up a loiterer's melancholy; and when
In a summer night against an open casement
Rustled along the balustrade the play
Of hands and voices, the illuminated gallery
Sounding with those lost and wooded flutes
Breathed out the subtlest perfume of young love.

But the crunch of a hob-nailed boot
Has a resonance all its own
Crisping a summer day with winter
Confounding the season,
Whether the foot
That shatters the red-clay tiles
Be Punic, Lombard, Hun,
The ravishing tread that hunts for loot
Be Visigoth or Canadian.

Ransacked now. The boots track upstairs and down
And in my lady's chamber. Rivered and ravaged
The stairways, drifting with table-cloths, withered letters,
Splayed, worm-spliced leaves of ancient wisdom,
A fragment of a children's hobby-horse,
All, all adrift with the flotsam of four centuries.
Was there some vileness lurking understairs,
Infection curled in the bud before it flowered,
That brought this dreadful cleansing on the house?
Say, rather, with a level voice, that the corpse
Of a dying house like the corpse of a man is vile;
And many a cause of death remains obscure.
But dying it is. Death in its brains and loins.
The fowler has loosed in the loft the doors of the cages;
The dove-cote, where crossing wings would silver and glide,
Deserted, presents only the guano stare of vacuity,
The birds have vanished like thoughts from a calcined skull.
And in the bowels of the house clot deadly humours,
The surfeit of garlanded years kept locked in the dark,
Furs, faience, crystal, silver, jewels,
A fistula soon to be broken in exquisite riot.
Death, finally. The dark cornucopia
Where the patron past dropped treasure lavishly,
Is corrupted by its own confined effulgence,
Is fouled with droppings, with the harvest of decay,
Is dank as a well full of years, as a well full of leaves.

What should the bell in the belfry say
Where the Madonna in low relief
Blest and divided the ordered day?
This is the moment of stasis,
Secular, silent with unbelief,
And timeless as a wilderness.
The cords are broken. No grief
From a passing-bell
Tells that a time-brimmed villa ebbs away.

Mildness that holds its mirror to departing breath,
Whose feathered winds attend to whisper if
The villa lives or no, this sky of limpid mildness
Has been invaded time and time again,
Has suffered Visigoths and Saracens,
Scarred by catastrophe but still serene.
Untimely peace bends over the shifting field
Embracing, as it seems, the pain that wounds it,
Charming the air. Far up reconnaissance planes
Are motionless and hang on strings, while shell-bursts
Drift down-wind and milkweed parachutes
Flower silkily. O calm entelechy
In which the soldiers on the tower are held!
Entelechy of silken peace and light!
That fastens actors on the lofty stage,
Emerged from winding ladders to this moment
By a dank trap-door. On history's monstrous back
(Their instruments set up to scan the future
And plot the guns in parallel) they ride
As harpooners a moribund leviathan,
Dabbling their feet in the crisped light that curls
Everywhere evenly, steadily; and sail scot-free,
Sail where the sun is scotched and quickly healed.
Surely this is not out of God's grace,
Where soldiers and a dying tower are lapped in peace.

The doves that death has dispossessed
Cling to the outward wall.
They will be scattered wide and lost.
Peace will come, if it come at all,
As an exiled bird with wounded breast.
The waves so rough
On the angry fields that truce
Can only fall
Like a prismed tear on a ravaged face.

Gaze deeper, then, still deeper into this limpid sky
Till the even grain is refracted into garish fire,
Stampeding, raging from the dark corona;
Fire-falls and veils that scythe and sway; cascades
Of blazing vapour when the heavens open;
Insinuating flames between the bricks and cornice,
Picking the bones of villas, skulls and voices,
Consuming ode and palinode and elegy,
Eating the salvo-smoke of human aims.
This will appear — though not to the theodolite
The soldiers swing or to a dying house —
Perpetual fire where lives like salt are spilt,
Fire where the earth is burning like a bush,
All-trampling fire by which new towers are raised,
Designer of wide-flowering stone and secret cells,
That charges through unrusted wheat
To burst its riddle in the kernelled ear,
That swirls and boils in the cup of the unripe grape,
That castles builds in the blood like ropes of sand,
That castles burns, and boils in a peasant's loins.
Violent the sea of fire the soldiers sail,
Too tightly closed in a luxury of flame,
Too softly stroked by a lion's paw
To see the blood in the flood of brightness
Or know themselves as the scars the sky devours.

Winds veer
And the weathervane veers
And the instruments are packed away.
But the crown with diaphanous veils
Of fire
Over the tower
And the trampled field prevails
And will prevail that far-off day
When other towers are circled by mild birds.

Persimmons

Just out of reach they glimmer like a globe,
A plaything for a boy, as round as promised pleasure,
But coloured with a different, luscious century,
Another world that riflemen make eyes at
From underneath steel helmets,
From underneath dry, spurious leaves they wear.

Trudging in single file through unsexed drought,
They whistle the fruit to modify the season,
With dusty voices supplicate green trees
To slake their thirst. But no streams break the heat,
No tantalizing, sweet
Drops stain the webbing of their discipline.

Still the thought of juice buds sweet on their tongues.
        Shoving
The lips of the beckoning fruit apart (a stinger
Like a wasp's probes deep for swooning nectar)
They sluice the sweetness out of their mouths till cool
Along their thighs they feel
A trickle of the girls they dream of loving.

At a momentary halt some break the branches,
Wolf down the fleshy liquor, which a few enjoy
But wonder what it is, a peach or orange?
And then a whistle blows. They fill their tunics
And slinging rifles, packs
And bren-guns, move forward into mortar range.

Tonight when digging parties comb the salient
Many a thin-skinned orient orb of sense,
A globe as soft as hand grenades are hard,
Will glimmer in untasted opulence
Crushed to the avid breasts
Of striplings, now wandering through a darkened orchard.

Reconnaissance in Early Light

See how he adjusts his scarf as we move off
And looking back along the waiting trucks,
Out of some distant past lifts up his glove
And smiles. The tawny sunlight falls archaic.

And stiffening with him in a ritual
Of battle we all get rolling, his scout-car leading.
As always, he is spruce and casual
And looks like someone going to a wedding.

He might be mated with the lion sun
Or with disaster, the paramour of beasts
Aprowl and coupling in this desolation
Where fallen tiles throw light on famished lusts.

The day waits. Is quiet as a ruined column.
Then, high up, air-bursts black as vultures in a moment
Suck all substance from the heavenly volume.
Listen! At last in the ditch the whine of shell-fragments.

And we sad lackeys wonder what comes next.
Is the ruin ahead or behind us? Does the road lead forward
Or back? His gaze alone is unperplexed.
He sips from this thin air some sacred word.

Through all his veins the sacrament of danger,
Discovering secret fires, runs riot. His hard
Eyes gleam with cunning pressed from smouldering hunger;
His coat burns sleek and lilied as a leopard's.

Whether some lucky chance has made him think
That glaze invulnerable or whether he puts
His pride before his life — and ours are linked —
Who knows? We only know we hate his guts.

The region is hermetic, though, and strange
And as he leads us to the holocaust
Our blood as well is volatized and changed.
Our dawning search is lit by wars long past.

Now as he crests the turret to sweep and lick
The landscape, snakes glittering back a wanton joy
Like a slick of flame from a hit petrol-truck
That in no time can ribbon through a convoy.

Crisp daggers naked in the daylight. Flash
Blue with Arcturus, crimsoned with Antares.
Diamonds, discharged from icy poles, gash
The frothed flesh with thrust of secret sympathies,

And, in our entrails twisting venomous truth,
Shriek that the star-wide world is desperate, desperate —
Fanged festival of stars from a serpent's mouth
Blazing us breathless to the Lion Gate.

An Incident

Arrange the scene with only a shade of difference
And he would be a boy in his own native
And fern-fronded providence,
With a map in his hand, searching for a portage overgrown
With brush. Slim he is as a moccasin-flower
With his throat open
To the winds, to the four winds, quivering,
Who alone by the worm-holed flower of the rose-pink house
Bears the weight of this many-ringed, foreign noon,
Shadowless, vast and pitiless.
Notched by the wedge of his frown, it takes no notice.
Light that, alive, would be pungent with resin,
Sapless, now weighs and ponders like limestone.

What is he waiting for
As he studies a map the colour of his youth?
Time stops and whirs in his ear like a hummingbird
As he gazes this way and that
For someone to relieve him
For someone to break through the thicket of his isolation.

In the silence
The grasshoppers crackle and crumble the summer
Between their thin wings
And their singing thighs.
And his head has begun to sing,
To sing with the heat.
Stampeding, his blood butts him like a bull-calf.
How should one so young have learned how to wait?

Ah! there is the relief.
A stray round has caught him at the nape of the neck
And splayed him flat on the earth,
His blood flung wide as a sunburst.

And the pink house, that eavesdropped
Through smoke-blackened holes to each palpitation,
Recovering its reserve,
Sucks in unblemished stillness;
While the wise light with petrified foliage
Having disposed of this awkward animal tremor
Again stands superb as a temple.

The Net and the Sword

Who could dispute his choice
That in the nets and toils of violence
Strangled his leafing voice
Enforced his own compassionate heart to silence,
Hunted no more to find the untangling word
And took a short, straight sword?

In this sandy arena, littered
And looped with telephone wires, tank-traps, mine-fields,
Twining about the embittered
Debris of history, the people whom he shields
Would quail before a stranger if they could see
His smooth as silk ferocity.

Where billowing skies suspend
Smoke-latticed rumours, enmeshed hypotheses,
And mad transmitters send
Impossible orders on crossed frequencies,
His eyes thrust concentrated and austere.
Behind his lids, the skies are clear.

Not that he ever hopes
To strike the vitals of the knotted cloud.
But, to the condemned, those ropes
At least let in the sun. And he, grown proud,
Among the sun's bright retinue would die,
Whose care is how they fall, not why.

The New Vintage

Wine of the new vintage they brought us
Bitter but the best they had
And by the wine or their kindness translated back to men,
Un-Circëd, we sat at ease in a spell of daylight
That we knew could never last. Though it did.
Day after day through amber richness dawdling
We hardly noticed the thin trickle of acidity
As one sun-caverned green-glass flask succeeded another
And the battle moved further away. It was an autumn solstice
Where we lay forgotten to play with children
In a vine-blessed house, a beatitude of husbandry
Discussing with the farmer crops and legends;
And returning rarely to our own sour dispensation
When tending the vehicles that sulked under leafy nettings.

Sons we were
Re-entered into a patrimony from which
Many of our fathers, grandfathers even, had been dispossessed.
And we moved through the house discovering family heirlooms,
Shocks of Indian corn that blazed from the rafters
And above the stairway tomatoes skeined in ruby clusters;
Or gazed through windows at fields and furrows
Where a woman switched on two milk-white oxen
Through bare fruit-trees, blue with copper sulphate,
That offered to the bare, blue sky fruits of repentance.
These things like the word of life we handled then.

But there is not a happy ending.
(Nor in the parable is mention made
Of the morning when the prodigal, redeemed and feasted,
Was sought in vain, once more a prey to bestial craving;
When his father found only a robe and mocking ring.)
One morning a signal came and in half an hour
We had loaded the vehicles and tied on extra gear,
Enough to make us at home in the winds and smoke
Where we would be coiled like wraiths through a new campaign.

We took the farmer's address and promised to write
And as he poured out the final viaticum
The new wine in our lying throats stung sharp and bitter,
There was no ray left of its sun-burnt, august sweetness.

He watched us to the last from the middle of the road
Staring along that barren tunnel as though down a rifle-barrel
Where the rifling circled in a glassy, baffling pool
Too deep with future for his aching temples,
A leaden pool that sucked down to he knew not what,
And shimmered with unheard-of consummations sterile.

The Nimbus

To dive for the nimbus on the sea-floor
    Or seek it in the sun
Calls for a plucky steeplejack
    Scaling sky's giddy ocean
Or dolphin-hearted journeyman
To swim from the foundered sunburst's roar
    With lost treasure on his back.

Ocean that slovens and sidles in vast
    Indifference, hides
In its sludge a wreath of drowning bells.
    Who in those tricky tides
Or up the slippery daybreak's sides
Can grapple the spices of morning fast
    That waste on the listless swells?

Smothered beneath a lowering ceiling
    All cock-crow crispness dies.
Bleary hordes are afraid to wake
    Into the mists that rise
From a palsied swamp where a marsh-bird cries.
Stranger, reconquer the source of feeling
    For an anxious people's sake.

Plunder the mind's aerial cages
    Or the heart's deep catacombs.
O daring's virtuoso, tossed
    Where the furious sunlight foams
Or through the instinct's twilit glooms
Return with the sunburst's glistering pledges
    As a garland for the lost.

A bittern rusting in the reeds
    Is startled, and through the mist
Whirs screaming. Now, if now only, come
    With the nimbus in your fist.
Strike, strike the rust like a rhapsodist
And burnish gold each throat that pleads
    For dawn's encomium.

A Man of Honour

When he awakened to himself, it was
Perpetual day. He must go on beneath
The midnight sun that hung its icy laws
Rebukingly about him, purging his breath.
Sharp lookout must be kept. No slackened pause
To sleep, no night to sip one drop of death.

Silently as an Arctic convoy steers
He must be stern and lonely, from the raked wings
Of his patrolling vices hide his fears.
At action stations always. One false move brings
A pack of submarines, one whimper tears
The tissued pallor where salvation sings.

Round many a crackling North Cape must he pass
Estranged from land, long centuries move
Snow-blinded, bewildered by the hectic compass,
Till at the valid pole at last arrive
His bearded honour frozen green as grass
And ashen eyes the sun burnt out, alive.

Elegy in the Romagna

I

How villainous the empty wine-vats grow
Here in the candlelight as I wait for fire-orders,
How cloaked and felted with shadows. The brown and bat-
Winged air has thickened to a brackish silence,
Brimming over old rakes and harness in the corner,
Filling the empty stalls, gathering and settling,
Swung from the storm on the gimbals of an ancient house.
So melancholy-still it is, so distant seems
The wash of shell-fire overhead, I hear
Adrift in the squandered grain the discourse of mice
Like filaments strung through this clouded calm,
Think I can even hear the cellar-spiders
Tugging from their guts their viscous webs.
I am the only other animal awake.
No messages. No new intelligence
Conducted to the low-plucked gloom unriddles
The suspense or signals changing weather;
Superior to clumsy hands, the fire-program
Continues, the shells interweaving, theirs and ours
In a maze of literal madness. The lines are quiet.
But in the smother something strains to speak.
In the clammy touch that wakes my throat there is
Entreaty, is entrance of an amnestied familiar,
Summons and recognition from a withering hand.
Commingled in the air the sweat and sighs
Of fifteen soldiers sleeping withers and grieves
About me. Exiled. Sour with the taint of exile.
Sour with the taint of surfeit. The heavy breath
Of men who have gorged all day on fear and danger,
Have supped with devils, dabbled in stews of corruption.
I smell the crooked nomadic ways they came.

II

Cut-throats, the shadows lead me with black knives
To vulnerable flesh. There the argument continues,
Lost seigneuries of childhood in wilderness
Engulfed, limbs gross with the leaves of darkness, and vines
Infesting the ruined chapel. My eyeballs are
Skewered forward to hang peering, shuddering. How far
The settlements are recessed! the candle almost out!
One of the sleepers moving in his sleep
Is tangled in a mess of gear, and groans;
One shows his back as brown as a tobacco leaf;
One sighs; one lies as though his neck were broken.

Dim spires far down the rapid river.

After the festivals of savagery (loud bodies
Writhing with vermilion), after flares and flames
And the stare of madness — this stupor of leather,
Where derangement of the subtlest tissues, still
Smouldering, creeps underground; and the breath
Of the burning bark, that innocence encased
And faggoted, seduces still in absence.
After the long traverse. The mind sunk sceptreless
In flesh till heat, cold, hunger, pain
As tetrarchs reigned, arbitrary usurpers.
After the ultimate rapids where the cargo was lightened,
The white caesura that stripped down longings
To the compass of these serviceable packs of greasy memories,
At the white mist where finally faded the bells —

Bells break the joists of swaying towers.

This rest in the meager feast of deep necessity:
Grain spilled on the floor, the empty wine-vats, dirty straw,
Enthusiasts and thieves together lying
Awkwardly in a bare thieves' kitchen.

Ache down, my eyes, along the closing vista
From prodigals and children pell-mell scattered
Through the choked pores and rivers, the paths blood-speckled,
Where animals fought infatuate and leaves
Are waiting for rain, to the shrunk estuary
By spires and settlements surrounded ... so distant!
The bay spread small and smooth as milk, a seed
Of cloud troubling the savage voyagers,
Trouble of birth in the winter-strangled tree
That can flower again and again through embarrassed bark
With buds and bells beclouded.

Bells buried in the earth and broken.

Leaves cursed with blood, voluptuous fronds of darkness,
O aboriginal heaviness in which
My gaze is limed and exiled! The wilderness
Laocoöns this ancient settlement.
Rusts and broods by the wall the heavy mattock,
The sickle tarnishes. And the husbandmen,
Cast out to see what wisdom there may be
In husks, stumble through trip-wires. If I should find
An emblem of order, a scythe that year after year
Mooned through the grass, disparaged it is
By shadows, in feverish growth sick metal sweats.
Or caves where the heart of the sleeping wine was warmed
And the sunburnt melody of summer extended
As a link in the seemingly endless garland of harvests,
They are gutted those caves, and hollow as gourds.
The song of the seasons is broken, the diadem
Star-studded, revolving in patient ecstasy
Over bent backs and rotated furrows, cracked.

Down fading spires stars trickle out.

The guns have shaken the stars from their sockets,
The weeping certainties of generation, cracked,
The voice of consolation, cracked.

Tonight the wilderness is here and everywhere.
And here sluggishly drifting (but seined by my candle
That sails mildly fishing through the dark)
Welters a gentle crew. Mangered in unease,
By sombre streams reduced, stripped naked,
Relation leaves them and identity,
Though childhood still is lilied in closed lids.
Dim to me

Dim spires for down the rapid river.

eyelids that fleur-de-lis the dark
Impeach the absent stars. O much traduced
And tarnished flesh, where guns and hungers peal,
Abandoned here beneath the blow of history,
But silvered still and still imperial
In the phosphored wash what quick life starts,
What filaments are spawned from misery?

III

Awake and conscious, and god-like so.
But the impotent god of a lost creation.
To pacify this brawl of whispers
My breath goes from me, and is impotent.

Spirits that weave the petals of the weeping flowers
Speak for me, speak natural powers,
While at the base of my brain
An ampoule of pity
Swells like a trillium.
Would break, would break in a cedar breath
From untarnished lakes and rivers,
Lakes of sweet water, skies of unsullied godhead.
Would suck in through the blanket at the door
Fresh breezes to this fetid lair
To wash all trace of cordite from the air.

Enters, though, as the blanket stirs aside
The scent of death, the sentinel,
Scent of dead horses and dead men,
O sickly sweet! The scent of nitre.

If there were stars and skies accessible,
A brightly tented system to bless
And diadem them whole like glistening hills at evening ...
If there were heavens to call to,
A promontory of comfort, some peak of comprehension ...
But dark, dark.

Guards of the house:
A dead horse with turds half-bulging from its rump,
A sergeant dead in the ditch, half-buried,
Green as his tunic. Verdigris blots him.
The whites of his eyes are scrawled with flies,
The hair of his head now dead and excremental.
These termini of nature picketing the nether pit
Impose a stern perimeter,
Guard the thick ferment, thought-threaded nakedness,
Clouding the fallible, fallen star in its own brightness.

In gusts redound on my diminished light
With foul air reeking, and send me back defeated.

IV

Absorbed. Given over to their silence. A membrane listening.
Misery is moving like the mother in a liquid.
'What will become of me?' Wash of the wilderness
Folds a thin filament, a white dissected nerve
In isolation. 'How like a knife in my guts
His glance has stayed.' Hangs in the air a moment
That cry, a dagger, slits open my ear. Thin fronds
Sharpened by scalpels sway in the brown bat-light.

Flesh has been cut by leaves of bitter laurel,
Tissue been cut away and the sheaths of brightness,
Environing lymph lapped up by fire
Till insidious fibres twitch their charged message
Nakedly, publish their lamentation. 'Lost.
O something that I lost as I was wandering.'
Struggling in the consistory of silence
To clothe their fallen anonymity
These limbs now never to be free from lesion
Cry through white nerves, cry seeking themselves
In a nameless ferment. Strand after strand I hear,
Phrase after phrase blown one way by the muffled wind.
And so the air is peopled. One breathes, 'I've seen too much.'
Another, 'Let me be lucky and be killed.'
These threads and hairs combed into a theme of nerves
Paint with so fine a brush the tympanum
Of a temple where the divinity is dying
I think of trees that sigh as the night wind rises
Of boughs lifting, quivering, green and black and grey
As bats and night-hawks pluck the sky's stretched membrane.
A theme of nerves, a downward branching tree
Where single fibres snap and link, are joined
In a system downwards, misery to misery linked,
Are interlaced in a light and delicate embrace.
These whispers harp to a proud king softly.
Joined ... joined ... joined in a tree of animal
Heaviness, of animal kindness.
I hear the sighing of a dark green tree.
White filaments compose a live green tree.
O I have listened long enough! My brain
Runs ruining down the desired descent, descent
Desired and paid for, down to the weedy dungeon
Where their cries are prisoned, where their breath is mist,
Where I myself am lying. Their cries are mine,
Their miseries thrill through my impoverished nerves,
People the dungeon of my bowels with fancies.
These are my villain fancies also.

No others would I have as my familiars,
No other company than this. In the ooze
And reeking vapours of a barren cellar,
I would have only such still and subterranean music,
Blind fingering of mice through destitution
And spidery tentacles as a covering for the brain,
A kind of comfort. Beneath a crumbling house
I sift the detritus of dreams with a goodly company.
In the heart-sick earth these clammy manacles,
These tendrils straggling in a turbid stream
Are furnishing enough as the night wind rises.
Rises to a muffled roar as the nearest guns
Resume methodical vituperation,
The whole house wheezing like a bellows,
And imprisoned tendrils, lifting, blowing all one way.

V

The candle starts and flickers
Interrogates the shadows, leaves them still more secret
The candle of the lord gone over to the captive voices
Enfolded in foul air,
Unkinged, uncrowned, and minion now
To every gust that blows the spider's wreckage.

Still the slow spider weaves.
And so make to trial. To imitate the spider,
From our unravelled tissues,
To spin an intellectual thread, no more
Mercurial nor more pure than this so precious crew,
That mounting, mounting, breaking, respun, as thin
As starlight, perhaps at last might clasp the upper air
And there restore relation and identity.
With webs dilating in lucid dialectic
Might jewel and justify limbs weak as gossamer,
Perhaps with eloquence of stars might stud
The drift of animal affection, and so make fast
A habitation in the wilderness.

Perhaps.
            But thick dew falls on my face.
I am gummed all over with a strange balsam.
I am sticky with sweat and with humankind
That fastens and laces me here. I am content.
Here is my place in a friendly heaven for a night
Where they have built a word- and star-less system
Perfectly. Our sighs like the milk
Of the milky way arch over us. Corrupted
Our lungs breathe out a new heaven of pity and concern.

The Green Man

Leaves twist out of his mouth, of his eyes, of his ears,
twine down over his thighs, spring out of his heels,
as he runs through the woods as a deer or an outlaw, or curled
up in moss and bracken, light speckling him feckless,
he watches the other animals, himself hidden
like an animal, although so strangely human
that if you surprise him you might think yourself looking
into the eyes of the mad but all-wise Merlin.

Boreal forest his most natural habitat
from the edge of our cities up to the tree-line
where at summer's end in the spongy Mackenzie Delta
he glides through pale yellowing poplars before the snow flies
or at Northwest River slips out of the spruce to play
with the huskies, chained on the shingle. His territory
spreads far and wide beneath the Bear. Morose
and frolic and savage his sports where the forests are.

But I have glimpsed him almost everywhere.
In pool-rooms and bargain-basements. In the glance of the dark
prisoner in the dock, not knowing how to plead,
passionate the criss-cross light that sifts through leaves.
In pale changing-rooms at the atomic energy plant
the young technician is changed into a sylvan man,
shadowed with mystery, and suffering from the sap
like a young green tree, quick thrall of earth and frenzy.

And quick he runs through my dreams, so quick and grieving,
to banish grey calculations of tomorrow,
to banish old gods with gay assurance,
impatient of bounds and all mere definition,
but sometimes himself a god, now minor, marginal,
now reigning sovereign over an empty tomb,
the incised leaves on his flesh now wounds, now blood,
now flame. The forest reeks now with vermilion.

There is a shade that glides beneath the skyscrapers
and makes those papery steeples soar and tremble
like poplars in the breeze, a green man's shade
who came before Champlain, green traveller, trader,
debauchee, wearing around his neck
gull's feathers and four new sweetwater seas,
interpreting the woods to Europe and Europe to
the woods — till finally he was cooked and eaten.

His taciturnities were our title-deeds,
his heart divided food that our hearts have fed on,
so many morsels from that seething pot,
some for the merchant princes in their lofty
boardrooms (a long long way from poor Étienne Brulé!),
but more for more ravenous hunters through other wastes,
lost, lost, and wild in utter inner dark
where the hunters and the circling hunted are the same.

And so I circle on the green man's tracks,
allured, bewildered by the bright green shoots
and headsman's axe he holds, those baffling icons
(for all the subtle theories that I half believe in)
that lead me on and down. But past all doubt
there thrives an underworld where life and death
are woven. And it is bright and dark and savage,
as speckled and as rippling as a snakeskin.

Outlaw or god this cunning harlequin?
I feel him darkening my glittering veins,
he kennels in my loins, knows every crevice
of my half-breed heart, and yet eludes me still,
though rumours reach me of him fugitive,
laughing and drinking behind an empty warehouse,
disguised in rags, and tossing empty bottles
to splash and sparkle on the cindery railway-siding.

Scion of the undergrowth and underworld
but a prince of darkness in all daylight polity.
I could lead you on a perfect summer afternoon
into a clearing where the trees are still and lucid
and have you stare and listen till a rustle comes
of a serpent moving underneath the columns.
Light slows. Leaves tremble — with Marsyas' blood as much
as Apollo's brightness. Now break a branch, it bleeds.

Some nights and seasons are his own, and sacred.
Then dreams flow into the woods, woods flow
into dreams, the whole pent city dreaming of a carnal
wood, confluence that empties into the streets
with a scurry of leaves and carnival drums and flutes,
and torches that set fire to the leaves and the city, a blaze
of harlequin crimson, skyward, as quick he still winds
among the masquers mocking, a green man with green wounds.

Stragglers

Suddenly he stopped running.
The air was breathless, spiked with thorn,
oak-leaves rattling from dead branches,
the scene so ruinous
a king's crown might have been found on a bush.

All he could feel was cold and pain.
Touch he had discarded like an empty cartouche-
box. For a while he could hear the angry owl,
but now not that, nothing.
Cold had burned him down to the bone.

He stood stock-still, like a skeleton, waiting.
Where were all his companions?
the lovely disguises that he had deserted him one by one
since the *sauve-qui-peut* and terrible rout.
Could they ever rejoin him as stragglers?

They had left him—his crimson sensual coat,
his suit of leaves like a man from the woods,
even the rich filigree of nerves—
left him.... Or had he left *them*?
given them up as alms to the wolves?

He didn't know. He was waiting.
Then like caribou over the tundra
came shambling the rags of a former richness:
a coat that once had been sleek and scarlet
but weatherbeaten now, torn, tattered

and folding itself against the cold;
and another disguise in dull rifle green
that seemed to be full of menace,
seemed now a spirit of destruction only
shorn of its old wild ambiguity.

They wouldn't approach too close,
these and other familiar wraiths,
but hung in the air like gaunt ruins
of a wardrobe. And he was powerless
to call or summon.

But the air seemed suddenly milder.
If a bird should sing
or a breeze breathe lightly over his hand
a word might come that would allow them to sign
a sorrowful injured concordat.

Victory

after the statue by Michelangelo in the Palazzo Vecchio

You can see how much love has gone into the modelling of the
    young man's flanks
untouchable!
and the young man's eye so blank and sovereign
absorbing the world.
But how strong too the old man's head between the hero's feet
bowed, bent, but still unvanquished.
So a god might shoulder a world
and be full of longing.
And which is more terrible,
the young man's eye or the power and knowledge in the old
    man's shoulders?

A Radiance

in memory of my sister, Elizabeth Josephine

How you still shine!

I see you
sitting on the dock to dry your hair.
A canoe of mandarin red in the hot sun blazing.
Towels. Paddles varnished and gleaming like fish scales.
As mink play on the rock, and I swim lazily on my back
and (moving in and out of the scene) look back
at the mink, and the canoe, and the paddles, and a birch-tree
white and green under the clear blue sky, and you under the birch-tree.
And when I climb out on the dock a few minutes later
and ask about a bruise on your arm
all you say, easily, lightly, is, 'I bruise easily.'

(You are what I can never be forgiven,
stronger than I, more easily broken.)

I see you
(now I am seas and continents away)
paddling alone far out in the open
of our broad sweet-water sea, the waves gentled
by the summer sun, and silky, sea-green
over the undulant shoals, farther and farther out,
(so you said later), with the thought beginning
to form of not returning, the canoe lapsing and lisping
over the gentled waves, you guiding its light sweet will
with your strong sweet will, not knowing yet what it was
or where it would carry you. But returning at last
through the shoals
while you still could make out the beacons.

(I the only one who could have saved you,
I failed you.)

I see you,
your absence in the rooms you made your own,
fresh, cool, immaculate, like lily-of-the-valley,
a spectrum now blended into perfect whiteness,
untainted by the tell-tale streaks and stains of madness
as I sit down to take an inventory—
an inventory of pain and loss and absence.
In the winter sun, straw-coloured matting.
Grey walls. A polished walnut table.
Your records,
the unplayed music rising, blending, into silence,
everything left as you would have it left,
and a deafening silence round the boxes of my letters that you kept.
(Even our handwriting was the same,
my hand that could have saved you.)

Now my eyes close
or almost.
My pupils close to pinpricks.
The rooms drift up with snow.

I see you in the snow,
great February drifts where you had walked alone,
snow white as morphine, merciless,
great billows of it where you were drowned, your hands
and feet sucked under, mortified, white sheets
drawn level with your sunken eyes, clouds
that fell on you, on your eyes, your lustrous hair.
Is there some realm of mercy in the clouds?
some hands into whose mercy I might yield you up?
some realm where I might be forgiven?

So we are told. And so I falteringly believe.
For as I falter on I see you shining still,
death's matchless bride
still radiant,
radiant beneath a canopy of swords.

Arthurian Enchantments

So, he had his own standards of splendour, and some few inklings
as a poet. But what of the prime stuff of poetry — words?
Start with a boy engrossed in 'King Arthur and His Knights'
and let that sink in until he is hardly aware of the residue
lost in his bloodstream. Now he has left knights in armour far
behind, their crests, plumes, mantlings, streaming in the wind;
but he still likes a style of military dash and crispness,
with hints of heraldry, of tapestry, of ancient music.
He agrees with Nabokov that 'The enchantment is everything',
although he has almost forgotten Merlin and Morgana le Fay.
But even now is he sufficiently wary of chivalric adventures
undertaken for the flimsiest of reasons — or for no reason at all —
adventures that lead deeper and deeper into the romantic wood?
Even now does he realize that those wounds were sometimes for real?

Reading the *Iliad*

The one thing certain is that we're all going down to defeat.
You can't win. Death, even a quiet death, will see to that.
Reading the *Iliad* week after week with a wise master
who would insist that Achilles was 'born to so short a life'
and that Hector knew that 'sacred Ilium must parish', a master
who had heard of no dispensation that could change that lot,
who accepted it, welcomed it, rejoiced in it, but believed
that it still mattered enormously to try to make something of it
and that all ages could be, should be, heroic ages —
ah, there was something to stick to your ribs, hard-tack
to keep in your knapsack for whatever event might come.
The marble face of the blind old rhapsode of Chios
fades into the face of that long-dead master of his youth,
a weathered urn whose tears had all been turned into wine.

A Head Found at Beneventum

Begin with the likeness of a young man's head on a coin,
as if he were perhaps the Antinous beloved by Hadrian,
and let that grow into a bronze head, more strongly and subtly
modelled, the eyes deep set and heavy lidded, looking
either inward or out toward some unknowable future,
a little like the bronze head found at Beneventum
and now in the Louvre. And then bring all that to life
in the figure of a young American with the gentlest eyes
in all the world, a fine oarsman, but deep into Proust,
Joyce and Mann, always *disponible*, always open
to what the world had to offer, but always reserved,
always sure — a little too sure — of his own innocence.
The hooks went in very quietly. As no doubt they did
when Hadrian lost his heart and head to Antinous.

A Nightpiece, of London in the Blackout

A wash of greatcoats circling about the foot of Eros
dethroned. Of nameless and almost faceless figures in the dusk,
drawn from a dozen countries, but all homeless, solitary,
adrift, uneasily on leave for a few brief hours or days
from history and its iron formations — or else deserters from them.
And a sombre sky, that's careless of the heart's elections
but carelessly forgiving of every anonymous encounter,
a sky quivering to a subtext hidden beneath the greatcoats,
tissues and textures throbbing with their own imperatives
(which might be gross or pure, promiscuous or crazed with love,
or both), with a thousand different objects and inflections,
that yet transmit a single impulse to the indulgent air,
a deep pulse of loneliness and outright lust and longing —
to share their nakedness with someone. Now! Tonight!

Two Views of Army Headquarters

It was like a Renaissance palace, he would tell his London
friends. And by that he meant that its corridors and conference-
rooms, even its gables and clustered chimneys, were informed
by the presence and virtue of a single man, as they might
have been by the presence of the prince at Urbino or Ferrara;
that his authority invested it; that its secrets were made darker,
its decisions more final because of his passionate intelligence.
The General (whom he was so proud to serve, who bore on his shoulders,
not only crossed swords and crowns, but life-and-death responsibility
for victory and certain loss) gave it his impress, coloured it,
from its sentries and clerks to its brigadiers, from its cellars
to the top of its parapets. At the time all that made it magical.
But now, compared with what followed, it seems rather flimsier,
more like a castle that a child might have cut out of paper.

Below Monte Cassino

Having had too much sex the night before for a man
over sixty, he feels a dull ache in the small of his back
about the size of a pie-plate, and suddenly remembers
(as he urinates into the toilet-bowl) dead
American boys in a field below Monte Cassino
and how surprised he had been as he picked his way
forward (avoiding the bodies as best as he could,
scared shitless of trip-mines and shoe-mines and glass-mines)
by one dead boy lying face down in the mud
with his arms and his legs flung wide and one big wound
in the small of his back about the size of a pie-plate,
having been caught there by a fragment of mortar-fire—
surprised then, and still surprised now, that what was
oozing from the wide wound was, not blood, but shit.

The Haystack

It doesn't take a Hiroshima to burn a man to a crisp.
A haystack will do. And what could be more bucolic
than that? And you get tired of sleeping in cellars or slit-trenches,
so why not behind a haystack that has simmered all day
in the warmth of an Italian September sun? But at night
the jackals are ready to spring, the German eighty-eights,
with their high muzzle-velocities and their low trajectories,
so that the haystack ignites like a torch and a gunner is burnt
to a crisp. How far back was that? thirty years? forty years?
He doesn't remember. He only remembers the stench
of fear, his own fear, and a grey army blanket, and a young
sunburned back alive on the banks of the Volturno,
then burning, burning. By dire subtleties such as these
he was being prepared for the carbonization of cities.

The Black Panther

He wakens to a tightness in his chest—
bronchitis? emphysema? lung-cancer?—
he doesn't know, but as he pads about
the flat to shave and make himself some breakfast
he feels a strange familiar in the darkness
there, a shadow mordant and malignant,
a something fanged and clawed that bides its time
and meanwhile pads about like a caged animal—
like something seen years ago in Singapore
on exhibition to the riff-raff at a pleasure-ground,
eyes blazing, muscles tensed, coiled, cramped,
the wooden bars could hardly hold it—that caged
marauder now turning into haunting image,
death the black panther now rustling in his rib-cage.

Emblem

Wild orchid, veined with tenderness,
that reaches down to glacial rock
past moss and rotting ferns and pine-cones
and the droppings of porcupines, raccoons.

This your just signet, seal and impress,
a moccasin plant on granite growing,
pink in the sun-shot shade of June,
frail trumpet, satin-smooth, and clear.

A flower, so fragile, soon will fade.
But while it lasts its fine-meshed membrane
both holds and hides a veined perfection,
a slipper that a prince might search for.

This emblem of the sensitive
and strong, triumphant short-lived song—
for you this emblem will not fade
but blazoning be and heraldry.

A Northern River, with Figures

Logged over, and then burnt over. Till all that's left
are scrub pin-oaks and jackpine over bare rock,
a scruffy landscape to serve as the high surround
for this river running down from Six Mile Lake.

But it brings with it sand and clay, sluiced down
by the spring run-offs, to make sandbars at its mouth
and to deposit a deep bed for the thread of the stream
and deep fertile banks for the summer vegetation.

That comes as the high season of metamorphosis.
Now it glides through a sweet cocoon of leaves,
past alders, and poplars, and towering birches —
a green palisade that quite blanks out the granite.

And the banks now are rich with Joe Pye weed,
great stands of it in abundance yard after yard,
their heliotrope flowers and tall purple stalks,
stiff, bending only a very little in the breeze,

but yet voluptuous, luxuriant, triumphant,
as though the whole scene had been transposed
to a different latitude and the kingfishers' clacking
to herald the canoe were now tropical, amazonian.

(Who Joe Pye was, seems to have been forgotten.
Some medicine man, I suppose, who was the first
perhaps to decoct from this imperial purple
an elixir of medicinal balms and balsams.)

The scene-shift could hardly be more fictive.
But it's not something longed for, imagined, not even
something achieved, but something simply bestowed,
a gift from the spring freshets and the strengthening sun.

And that was the way that you entered my life,
gratuitously, not as something I richly deserved
for hard work, or suffering, or labours accomplished.
You came very quietly to blot out the granite.

I don't like to recall all the years that my life
ran through bare rock. Perhaps some might say
I made it that way myself, raised up its ridges
and whalebacks, made it even that way for others.

Perhaps. Yet I doubt it. I prefer to arraign
the wars, and rumours of wars, and wars' aftermath,
leaving deep scars and parasites. That was what
ruined 'a fine gentleman', almost ruined a poet.

It was you who gave me back summer, and ease,
and refreshment. A blithe featheriness of leaves turning
in the wind. A playfulness of green foliage hiding
grey rock. A lithe natural heroism of rippling

strength as if to fulfill a tree-spirit's dream.
A sweet elixir from such savage flowers decocted
as would medicine me back to wholeness, coaxing
my foiled valiancy to turn once more to the sun.

Flames, at the Beginning

I am burning your letter, as you asked me to.
In the light through the window it flames up like a great
        gold chrysanthemum.
Our love will flourish like that, extravagant and secret.

According to La Rochefoucauld

Constancy in love is of two kinds
                                        wrote terse La Rochefoucauld.
One is like an inexhaustible spring and comes out constantly finding
new things to love in the one you love. The other comes from
making it a point of honour to be constant. (And you might want
to remember that he was a soldier before turning aphorist.)

So the parts are evenly divided between us, dear comrade-in-arms.
But my part is far easier than yours. I'm constantly finding
in you new things to love, new drolleries, new endurances.
While you?
            Free as you are, and as I want you to be,
I'm afraid there must be many times when constancy for you
comes down to a point of honour.

Passacaglia

I love it when you tell me you love me. But there's no need.
I can tell that from the way you move when we're alone.
But what's harder is trying to figure out *why* you love me,
someone so weatherbeaten, so morose, so footsore and heartsore
from the journey, living only from day to day, accustomed
to loss and disappointment, hardly expecting anything else,
with hardly anything more than a soldier's low horizons.
But even now that you've utterly changed the prospect,
and (with a little help from me) broken down my dour carapace
and mollified the proud flesh round my wounds, there's still
plenty of scar-tissue left. So ... why? But the very question
may well be rather ridiculous, a hangover from a different
life and a different habit of discourse, before the old terms
and categories were radically altered. As well ask perhaps,
Why are the upper staves of the passacaglia in love
with the seemingly sullen bass? Or, why is the aria
in love with the accompaniment? The free-floating tenor
or coloratura aria, that has a wealth of playful
or spirited *fioriture* and brilliant cadenzas; the accompaniment
that simply seems to rock back and forth, back and forth,
and has little more to say for itself than that. Yet together
they make something out of this world, with its own pulse
and breathing, different from ours, yet leading us on,
showing us the way into a delectable transient clearing,
the skies a halcyon azure, but with traces of passionate scarlet.
Now I'm learning to stop asking questions and simply
to listen to the music. And it's full of surprises. Sometimes
it's rowdy with kettledrums, sometimes placid as a sunlit lake,
sometimes as deftly inconsequent as a long poem by Frank
O'Hara. But whatever it is, you make it all *cantabile*.
I waken to ethereal music, to bird-song as though
flutes were conversing with oboes, or to murmurings,
raptures, that seem even more heavenly, more profound.
I look up surprised, to see that there's a helicopter overhead,
trailing a long sign that reads lazily, 'No more questions, please.'

Strip *gloire* and *grandeur* from their place in the pediment.
But heart's blood is still needed as much as ever before.

Topple the ridiculous Sun King from the height of his pedestal.
But what is a *cour d'honneur* without heart to defend it?

It's the heart's blood of courage, with its systole and diastole,
that runs through and supports everything mankind has made.

The minuet, the flowering cadenza, are nourished by heart's blood.
The artist, as much as the athlete, depends upon heart.

What of the other manifold virtues? They would be as nothing
without the circlings of courage sent to sustain them.

It takes many forms, this primal animal virtue,
but a soldier's honour may stand as a blazon for them all,

whose calling demands of him courage, endurance, loyalty,
and the ultimate commitment to be ready to stand and die.

So the far-off fanfare may fade but is never uncalled for.
Even peace-keepers still need to be clad in the soldiers' virtues.

On a Path Behind the Hotel

He has picked himself up again and again
after being knocked down more times than
he cares to remember. And now here he is
idling along the pathway behind the hotel
high above the lift-locks that lead to the canal.

It's summer, and he's wearing a torn straw-hat,
and carrying a fishing-rod as if he'd just
climbed up after trying his luck in the river.
But nothing is simple behind those candid eyes.
Does it show? he is wondering. His questions are legion.
Is it a blessing of sorts or will it spoil everything?
How large is the band of those who are like him?
Have there been times and places where things
were different? He doesn't know how to answer.
Or to define what it is that separates the courage

he needs from the cowardice with which he's been branded.
He is waiting for someone. But who? That too
is concealed from him. It might be a sadist
or brother, a pilgrim or dissolute wanderer,
a face now muffled in weeping or clouded in beauty.
If only there were a voice from a cloud to tell him
that Aeschylus, who was proud to have fought at Marathon
(so proud that he had it carved on his tombstone),
had no doubt that Achilles and Patroclus were lovers.
Or someone to sing of the Sacred Band from Thebes,
who over the centuries have triumphed in defeat,
beneath the stare of their heroic stone lion, the lovers
lying in swathes on the field of Chaeronec,
in a lustre that links love and courage forever
in swathes of fidelity perennially ripened to harvest.

Willow Trees, by Killarney Channel

Green willow leaves reach sinuously down like fingers
to fashion a green silk pavilion for lovers to sport in

as, earlier, catkins had silkily burdened the branches
with a soft flicker and flowering, burgeoning downwards

like light through a window on lovers undressing, speckling
their hummocks and hollows of nakedness, stippling them

as they advance, retreat, now shyly, now boldly, but never
with shame, or with anything other than compassionate lust,

till, overhead, what is created is a heavenly canopy,
something that is common and royal, sacred but natural.

There is room here for amorous couplings. And for the thin
wing-beats of butterflies, airy, ethereal, ephemeral,

within a green pleasance bathed in a tented transparency,
where sun mottled with shade calls out to androgynous angels.

But this is a trope that can move either forward or back
(and either languidly or strenuously from one side to another).

Your fingers as they search down the curves of my thighs, make
me remember green willow leaves and the light falling through them.

Your tongue as it ripples from side to side makes me think
of the sough of willow branches as they sigh in the wind,

of their taut springiness, of the strength of their pliancy,
of their relaxed stalwartness seemingly made for serious play.

It's from play of that kind that our union is formed, white-hot
and sacred between us, to burn at the core of our world,

while far at its outskirts torchlight carries the flame
through dark nerves and sinews, extending the bonfire light

till the flame dies down. And then blue skies. And a sea-blue calm
that now washes everywhere, to mirror the sky-blue of heaven.

About Douglas LePan

Douglas Valentine LePan was born in Toronto on May 25, 1914. His father, Arthur D'Orr LePan, a decorated World War One veteran and University of Toronto-trained engineer, had married LePan's mother, Dorothy Edge, in 1911. A bright child in the eyes of his parents, LePan outshone his older brother, Arthur, and his younger sister, Josephine. His association with the University of Toronto was lifelong: his father oversaw the buildings and grounds; he received his secondary-school education at the University-administered high school; and he earned his undergraduate degree at University College in 1935. A scholarship allowed LePan to spend the next two years at Merton College, Oxford. Returning to Canada in 1937, he lectured at his *alma mater* before obtaining a similar position at Harvard in 1939. There, he met Charles Olson.

War broke out in Europe in September 1939. Like many of his generation, he had realized by his late teens that 'war was now inevitable, and Canada would be involved, and I would be involved too.'[1] While in Boston, LePan tried to enlist with the Canadian Army and, due to his poor eyesight, was twice refused. By 1941, he found another way to serve. Hired by the Canadian Legion War Services, he sailed to England that October and in June 1942 became the Personal Advisor on Army Education to General Andrew McNaughton. The sole civilian among one hundred officers at Army Headquarters in Sussex, LePan developed comprehensive educational programs to keep the 120,000 Canadian troops under the General's command occupied productively while strategists awaited the opportune moment for Allied land forces to invade continental Europe.

By May 1943, LePan's duties passed from his civilian hands to those of an officer, and he was working for Vincent Massey at the Canadian High Commission. However, the 'ordinary Canadian soldiers'[2] he'd met haunted him. He asked himself 'why should they

1. Douglas LePan, *Bright Glass of Memory: A Set of Four Memoirs*. Toronto: McGraw Hill-Ryerson, 1989, 10.
2. Ibid, 42.

be going through the shit and corruption while I was sitting at my ease in my office on Trafalgar Square? I ultimately allied myself more, I hardly know why, with their common dying clay and with any distinction that could flower from it than with any distinction, however extraordinary it might be, that rested on rank and privilege.'[3] LePan 'decided that, if I could get myself enlisted, I would stay in the ranks.'[4] On McNaughton's advice, he volunteered for the artillery, and by mid-1944 was serving in Italy as a gunner in the 1st Field Regiment, Royal Canadian Horse Artillery, the oldest regular unit of the Canadian Army. While waiting to enlist in 1943, LePan met T.S. Eliot, through a letter of introduction furnished by painter Wyndham Lewis, whom he'd known in Toronto in 1941.

After the war, LePan joined the Canadian diplomatic service, first serving in London, where he met Elizabeth Bowen. Impressed by the 'sheaf of ten or twelve' poems[5] that LePan had shown her, she passed it along to poet C. Day Lewis, a director and senior editor at Chatto & Windus, which published *The Wounded Prince and Other Poems*, LePan's first book, in 1948. The same year, LePan married Sarah Chambers (they would have two sons) and won a Guggenheim Fellowship. His wartime experiences in England and Italy and his identification with his fellow soldiers gave *The Net and the Sword* (1953), his second book of poetry, and *The Deserter* (1964), his only novel, their substance. Both were recognized with Governor General's Awards; they are inarguably two of the finest books written by a Canadian about the Second World War.

LePan spent just over a decade in the employ of the Department of External Affairs, also serving in Washington and Ottawa, where he was seconded to the Department of Finance. He resigned from the federal service in 1959 to resume academic life, teaching at Queen's University and at the University of Toronto, first as Principal of University College and then as University Professor and Senior Fellow at Massey College. Though *Bright Glass of Memory: A Memoir in Four Parts* would appear in 1979, a demanding

3. LePan, *Bright Glass*, 42.
4. Ibid, 40.
5. Ibid, 131.

professional life left him little time for creative work. It was not until 1982, almost thirty years after the release of *The Net and the Sword*, that he published his third book of poetry, *Something Still to Find*. It was quickly followed by *Weathering It: Complete Poems* in 1987. LePan received the Royal Society of Canada's Lorne Pierce Medal in 1976 and was awarded several honorary degrees; he was made an Officer of the Order of Canada in 1998 on his death bed. He died that year on November 27.

In 1990, LePan shook up literary Canada's established impression of his work with the publication of *Far Voyages*, a book of love poems written in memory of Patrick Fabbri, who in 1985 died from cancer at thirty-seven; by then, the two men had enjoyed a more-than-decade-long relationship. Awareness of LePan's sexual orientation has since allowed for queer readings of his work, which provide insight into twentieth-century gay experience, especially during the decades prior to Canada's decriminalization, in 1969, of consensual sexual relations between two adults of the same sex. By the mid-sixties, LePan's marriage had deteriorated irreparably, but the couple maintained a household together until their youngest child had left home. They separated shortly after, in 1971.

LePan returned to the war in his final book, *Macalister, or Dying in the Dark* (1995), a verse drama about John Kenneth Macalister, whom he'd known slightly as an undergraduate at the University of Toronto in the 1930s. In 1943, Macalister parachuted into occupied France as a spy, only to be captured and, with a group of Allied prisoners, brutally executed after an attempt on Hitler's life in 1944. LePan concluded his literary career on a valedictory note that reprises a central theme: the idealism, valour and duty of men against conflict's horrific backdrop. As he wrote to his sons in the epistolary introduction to *Bright Glass of Memory*, 'the friends I had then in extremity were closer to me in crucial respects than any I have had before or since.'[6] *Macalister* recalls the motivations of First World War poet Wilfred Owen, who died a week before the Armistice and who wrote 'My subject is War and the pity of War.

6. Ibid, 4.

The Poetry is in the pity.'[7] While LePan's subjects were diverse, from reading the *Iliad* to canoeing through untouched wilderness, the pathos Owen felt is the pathos that LePan shared — and voiced in everything he wrote.

---

7. Edmund Blunden, ed., *Poems of Wilfred Owen*. London: Chatto & Windus, 1964.

A Bibliography

POETRY

The Wounded Prince and Other Poems. London: Chatto & Windus, 1948.

The Net and the Sword. Toronto: Clarke Irwin, 1953.

Something Still to Find. Toronto: McClelland & Stewart, 1982.

Weathering It: Complete Poems, 1948–1987. Toronto: McClelland & Stewart, 1987.

Far Voyages. Toronto: McClelland & Stewart, 1990.

Macalister, or Dying in the Dark. Kingston: Quarry, 1995.

FICTION

The Deserter. Toronto: McClelland & Stewart, 1964.

NON-FICTION

Bright Glass of Memory: A Set of Four Memoirs. Toronto: McGraw-Hill Ryerson, 1979.